DEC 14 1995

CHOPIN - Very Best
for piano

Frederic Chopin

(1810-1849)

Catalog #07-2028

ISBN# 1-56922-060-3

Printed in the United States of America

Produced by John L. Haag

Exclusive Distributor for the Entire World:
CREATIVE CONCEPTS PUBLISHING CORP.
410 Bryant Circle, Box 848, Ojai, California 93024

Photographic portrait of Chopin, age 38

CHOPIN - Very Best for piano

Contents

Assorted Works

Mazurkas

Nocturnes

Polonaise

Preludes

Waltzes

Caricature of Chopin (1840)

Chopin, age 37

Chopin at age 28

Pencil sketch (1847)

Bust of Chopin (1841)

Chopin at the piano, age 28

Chopin

A pencil and chalk portrait (1847)

Chopin at age 19 or 20 (oil on canvas, 5 1/2 x 9 inches)

Marble head of Chopin

Watercolor of Chopin at age 16 or 17

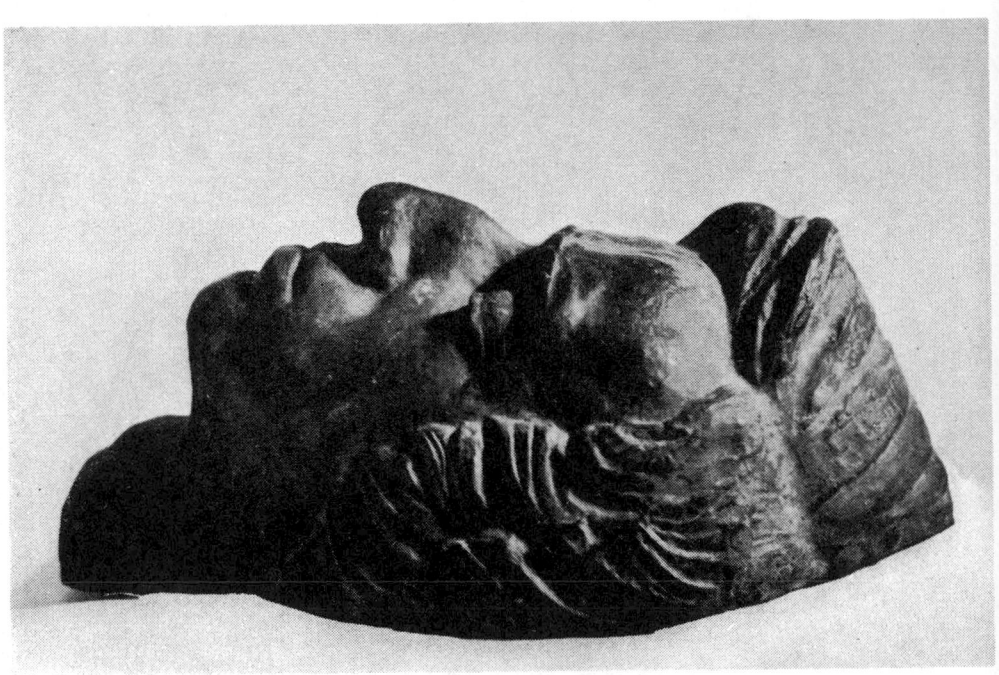

Bronze head of Chopin after the death mask (1941)

FANTAISIE IMPROMPTU
(Opus 66)

Frederic Chopin
(1810-1849)

Tempo I° (Allegro agitato)

Klindworth:

FUNERAL MARCH
(Opus 35)

Frederic Chopin
(1810-1849)

IMPROMPTU
(Opus 29)

Frederic Chopin
(1810-1849)

Allegro assai, quasi presto

PREMIRE BALLADE

(Opus 23)

Frederic Chopin
(1810-1849)

* In some editions:
  In manchen Ausgaben:

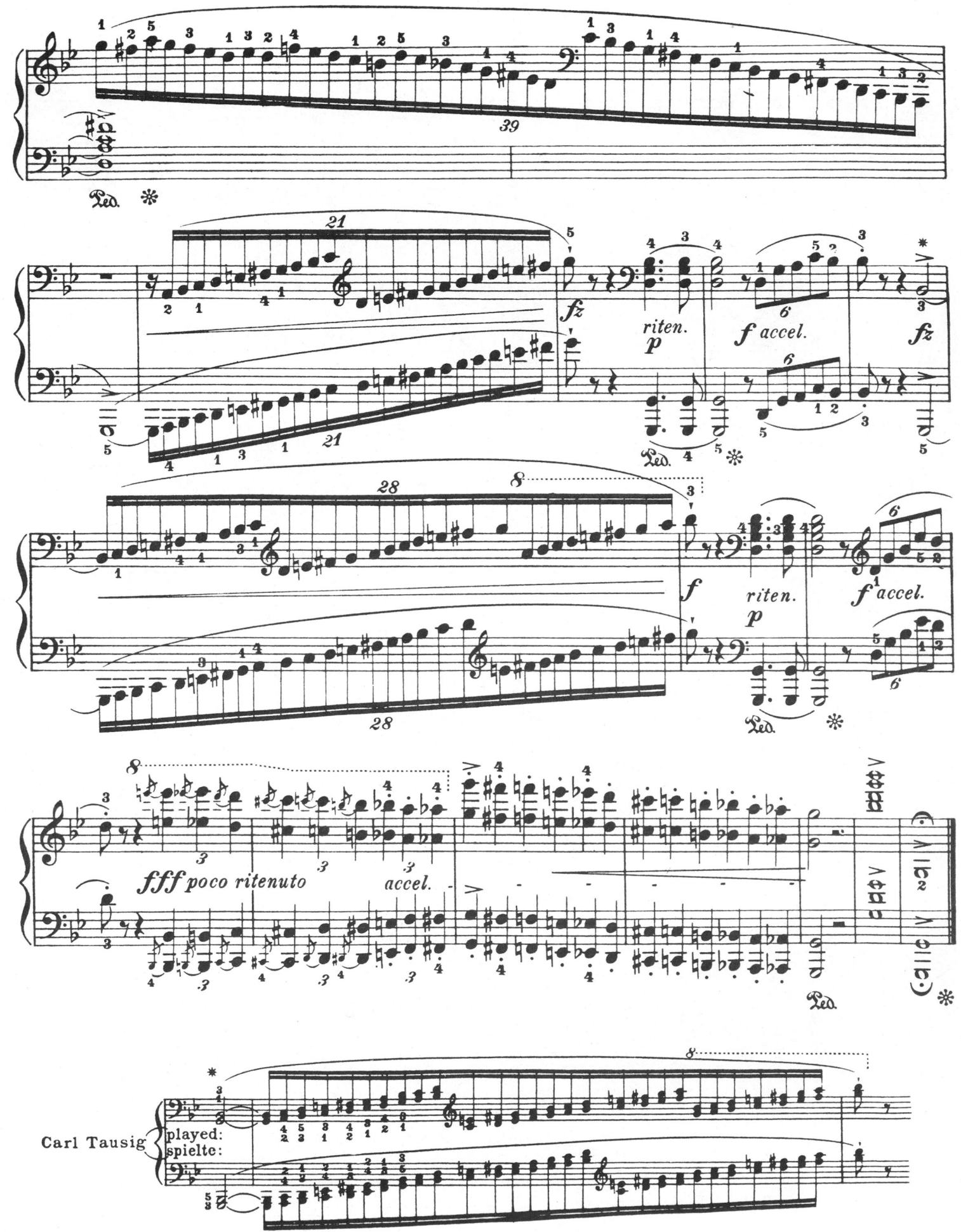

Carl Tausig { played:
spielte:

PRELUDE NO. 15
(Opus 28)

Frederic Chopin
(1810-1849)

Sostenuto

PRELUDE NO. 3
(Opus 28)

Frederic Chopin
(1810-1849)

*) Carl Tausig, who had a marked preference for a stretchedout position of the fingers, used the following fingering:

PRELUDE NO. 4
(Opus 28)

Frederic Chopin
(1810-1849)

PRELUDE NO. 6
(Opus 28)

Frederic Chopin
(1810-1849)

PRELUDE NO. 22
(Opus 28)

Frederic Chopin
(1810-1849)

CINQ MAZURKAS

(Opus 7 No.1)

Frederic Chopin
(1810-1849)

MAZURKA
(Opus 33 No.3)

Frederic Chopin
(1810-1849)

Semplice

NOCTURNE
(Opus 9 No.2)

Frederic Chopin
(1810-1849)

NOCTURNE
(Opus 27 No.2)

Frederic Chopin
(1810-1849)

NOCTURNE
(Opus 15 No.1)

Frederic Chopin
(1810-1849)

Andante cantabile. (♩ = 69.)

NOCTURNE

(Opus 37 No.1)

Frederic Chopin
(1810-1849)

NOCTURNE
(Opus 48 No.1)

Frederic Chopin
(1810-1849)

NOCTURNE

(Opus 55 No.1)

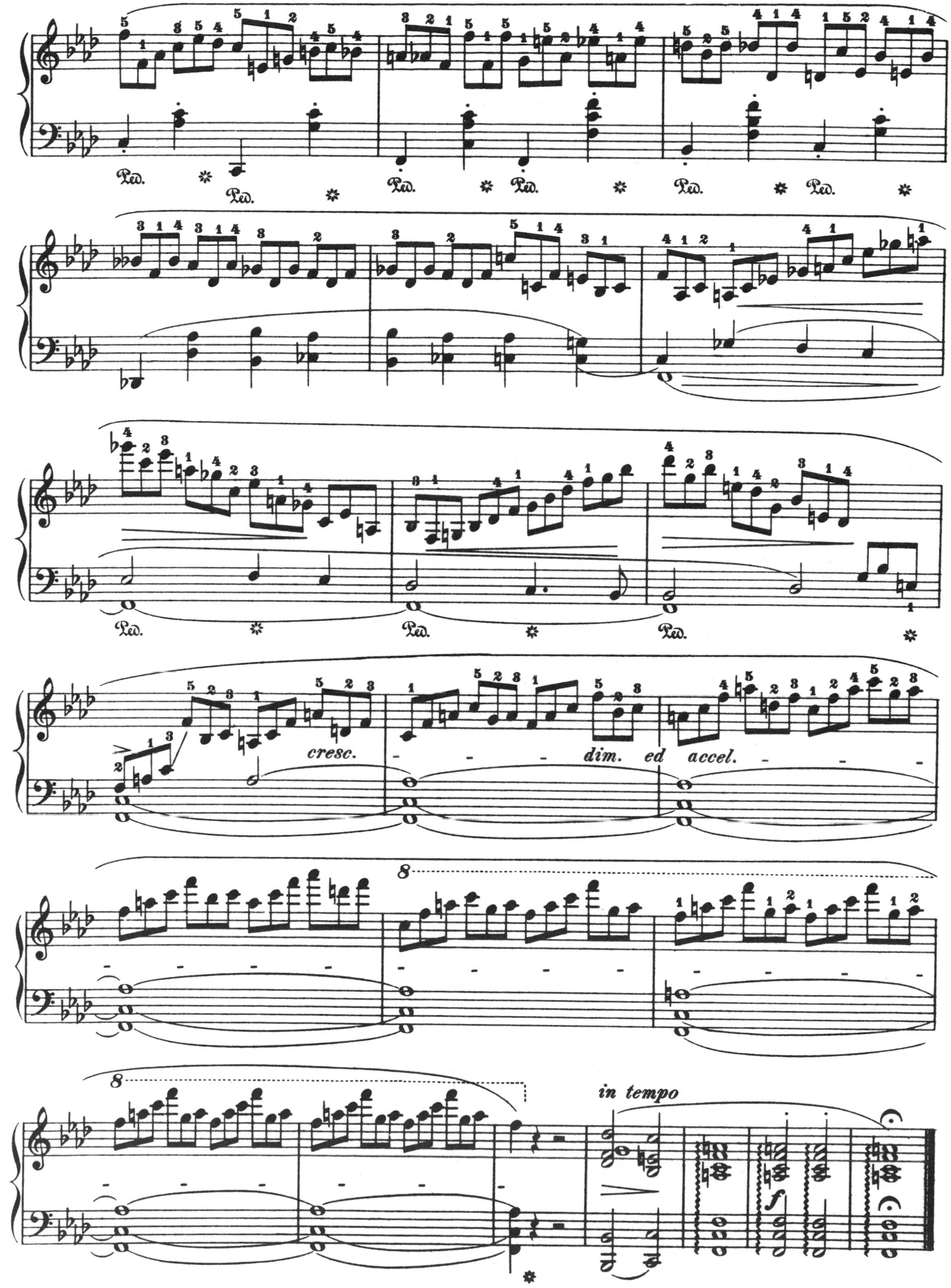
Ped.
cresc.
dim. ed accel.
8
in tempo
f

POLONAISE (Militaire)
(Opus 40 No.1)

Frederic Chopin
(1810-1849)

Allegro con brio.

POLONAISE
(Opus 40 No.2)

Frederic Chopin
(1810-1849)

Allegro maestoso.

POLONAISE
(Opus 53 No.6)

Frederic Chopin
(1810-1849)

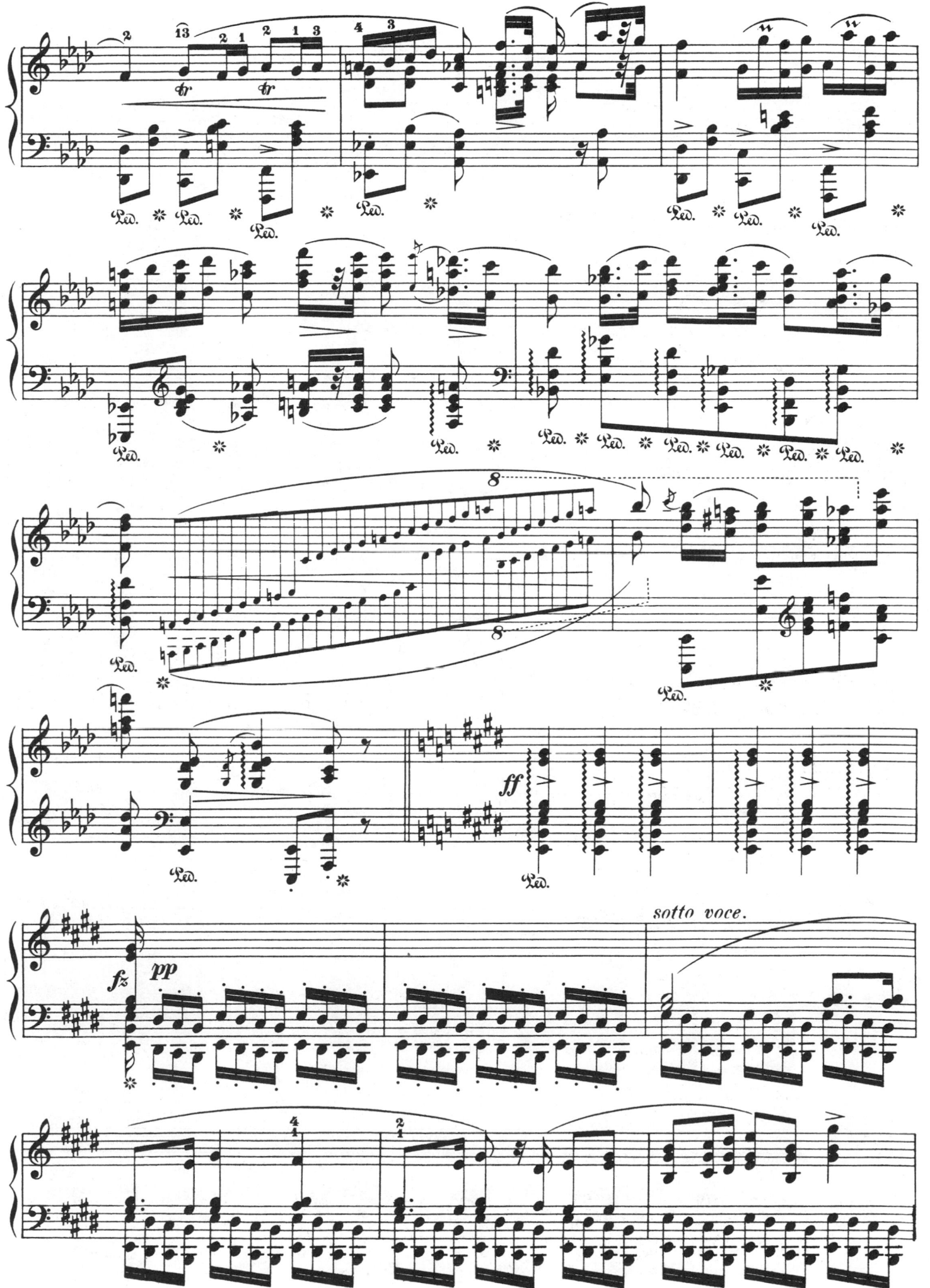

POLONAISE
(Opus 71 No.2)

Frederic Chopin
(1810-1849)

Allegro, ma non troppo. (♩ = 92.)

GRAND VALSE BRILLANTE

(Opus 18 No.1)

Frederic Chopin
(1810-1849)

VALSE BRILLANTE
(Opus 34 No.2)

Frederic Chopin
(1810-1849)

VALSE
(Opus 42 No.5)

Frederic Chopin
(1810-1849)

VALSE (The Minute Waltz)

(Opus 64 No.1)

Frederic Chopin
(1810-1849)

Molto vivace

VALSE
(Opus 64 No.2)

Frederic Chopin
(1810-1849)

Tempo giusto.

Più lento.

VALSE

(Opus 69 No.1) Posthumous

Frederic Chopin
(1810-1849)

VALSE
(No. 14)

Frederic Chopin
(1810-1849)

VALSE
(Opus 64 No.3)

Frederic Chopin
(1810-1849)

poco a poco accel. al fine